I0170897

A GARDEN OF
ORNAMENTS
COLORING BOOK

This book is printed on just one side of the paper
to avoid bleed through. If using markers it may be helpful
to place a piece of paper or cardstock behide the page.

To view samples of these illustrations colored by the author please visit
www.lovelyleisure.me

LOVELY LEISURE

ILLUSTRATIONS BY PAULA PARRISH

A Garden of Ornaments Coloring Book
© 2015 Paula Parrish

www.lovely-leisure.com

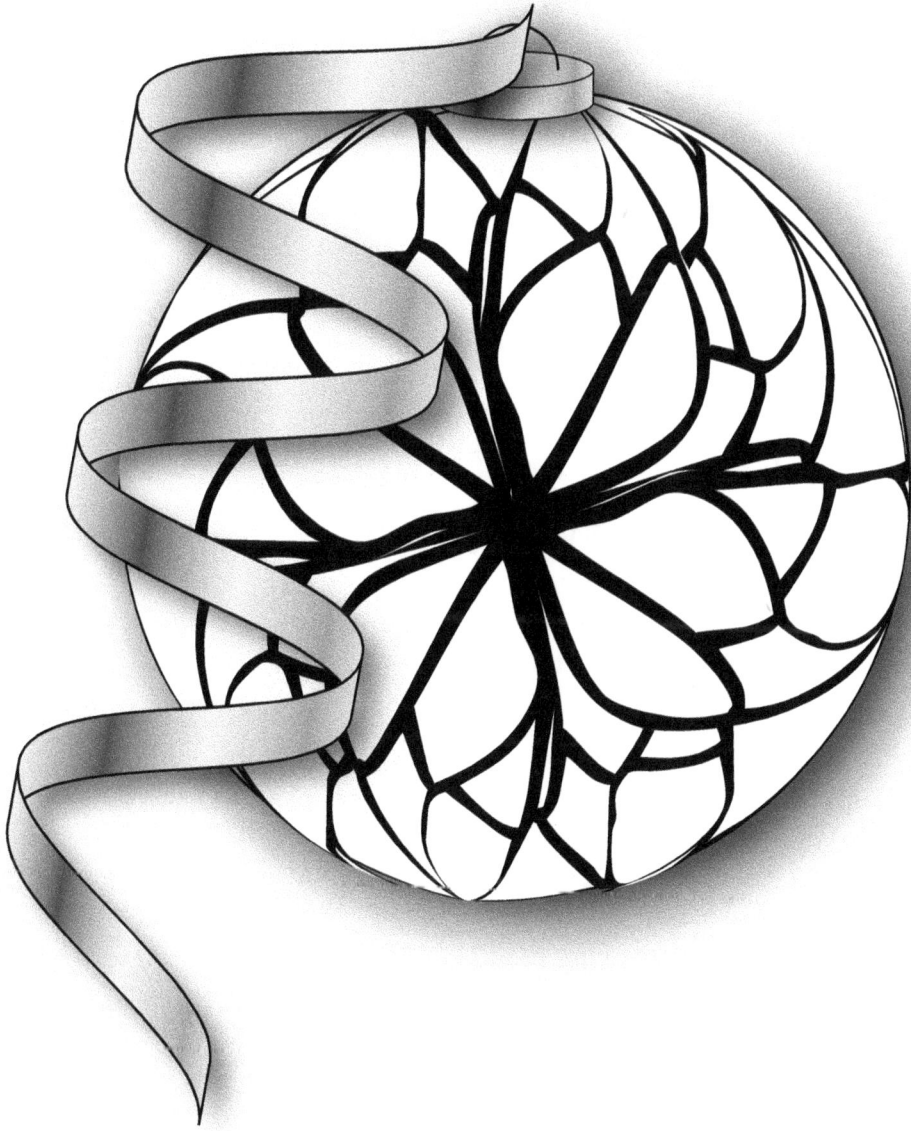

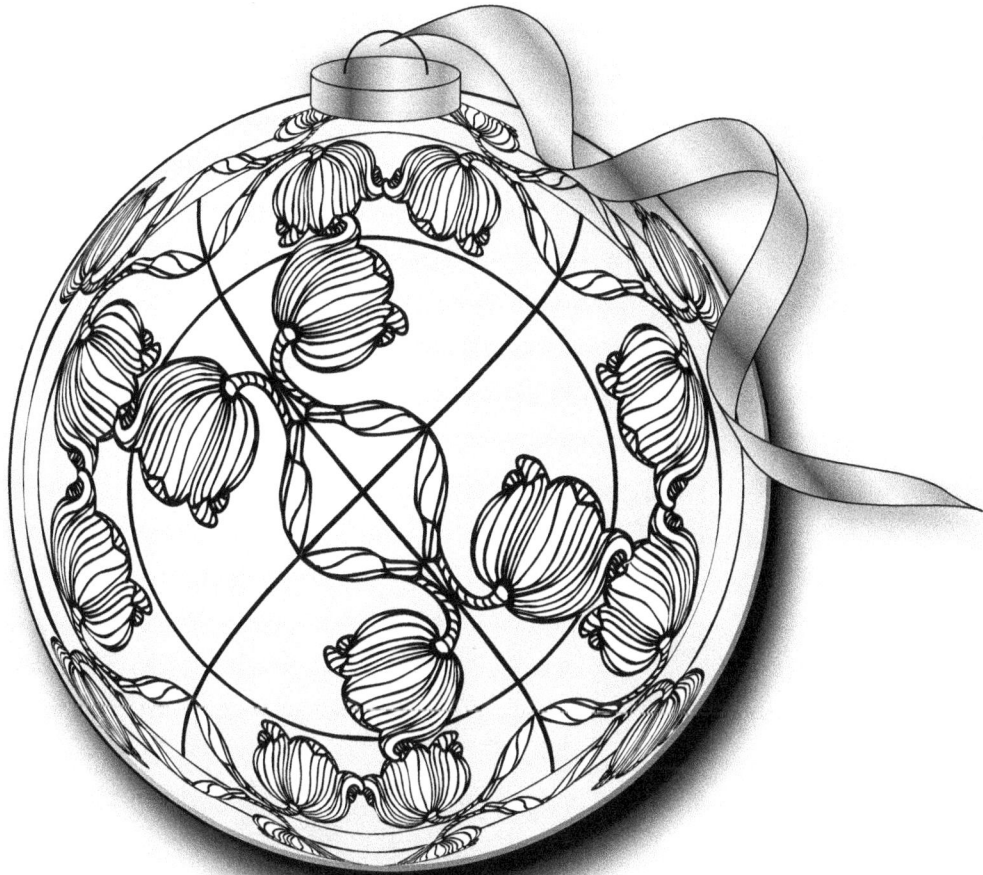

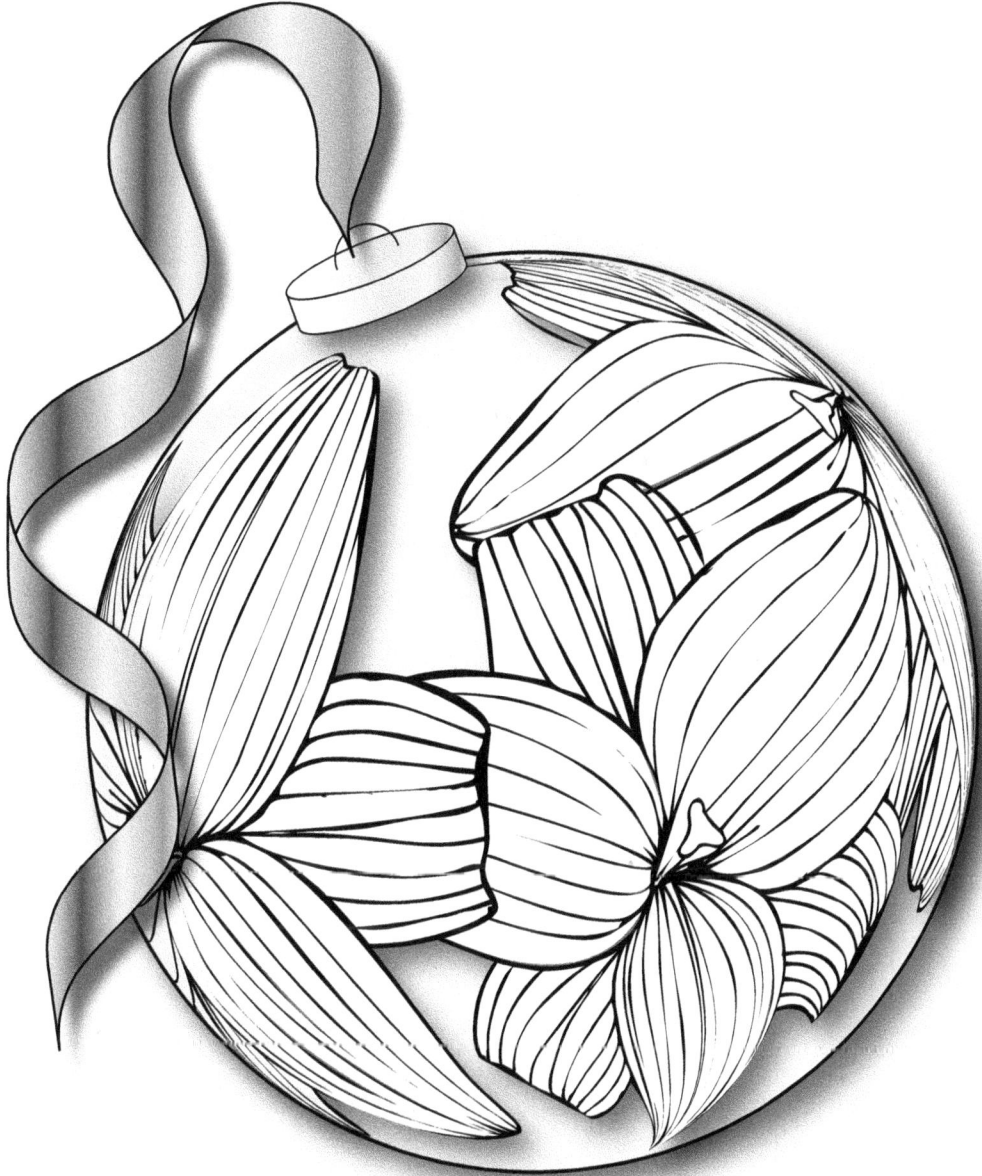

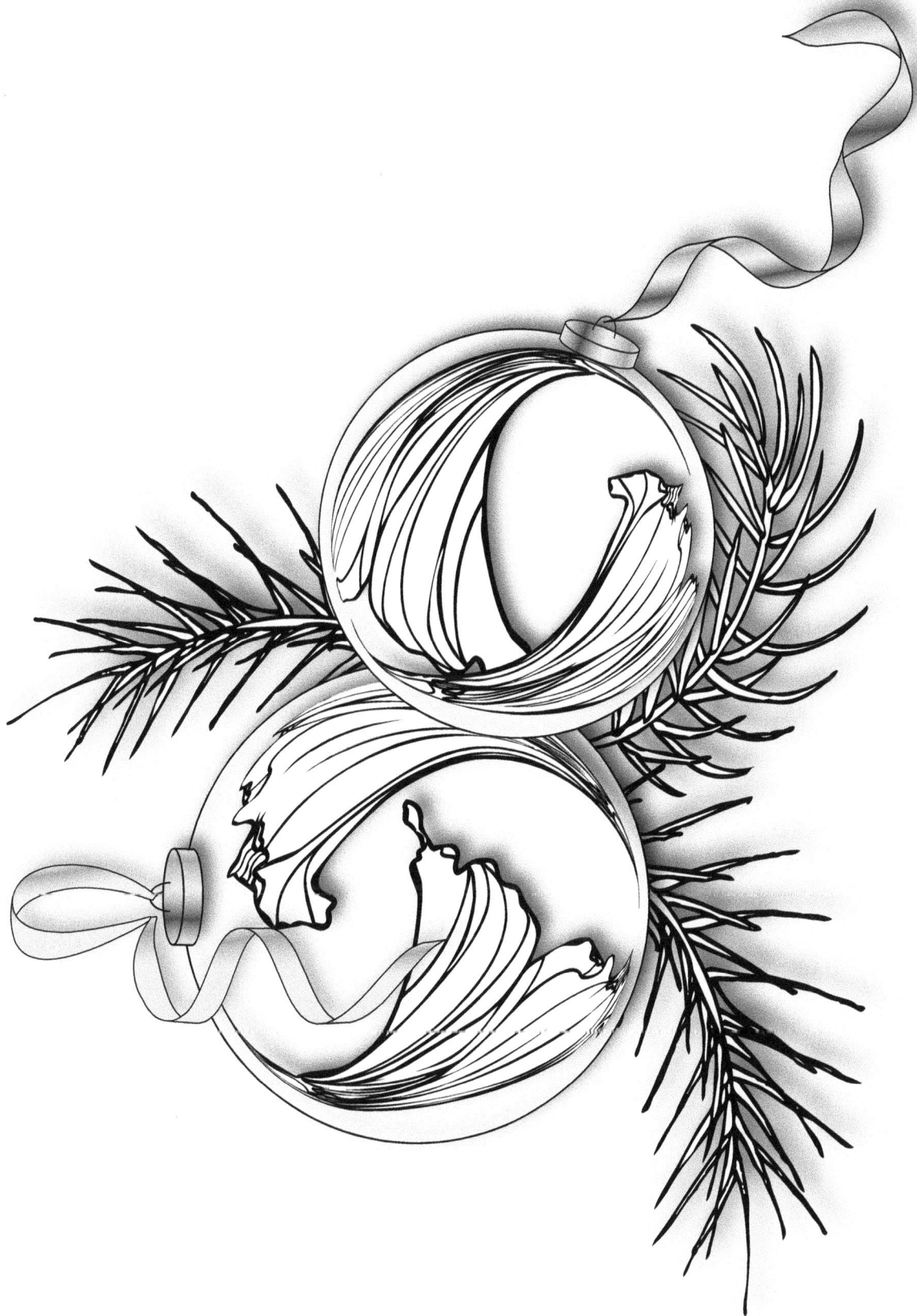

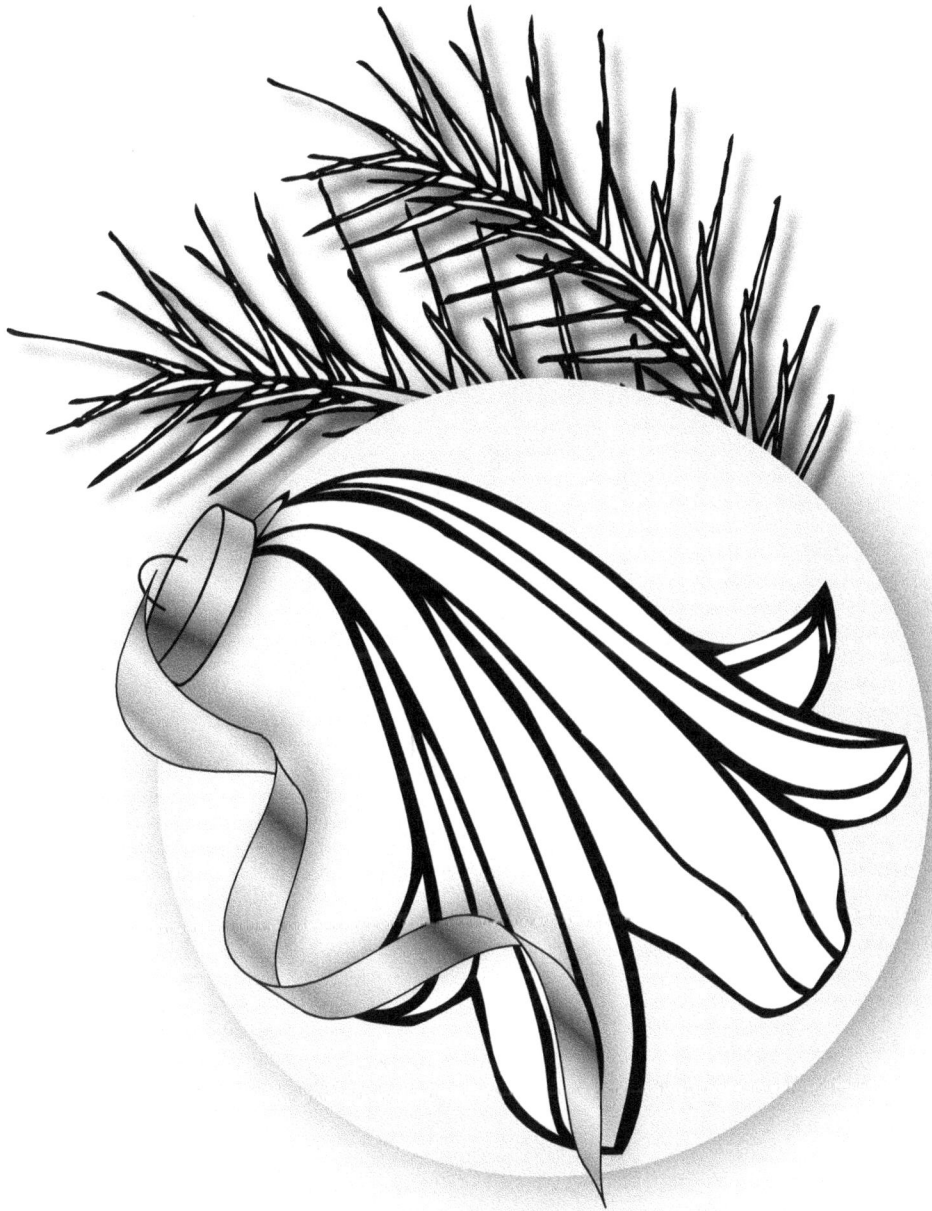

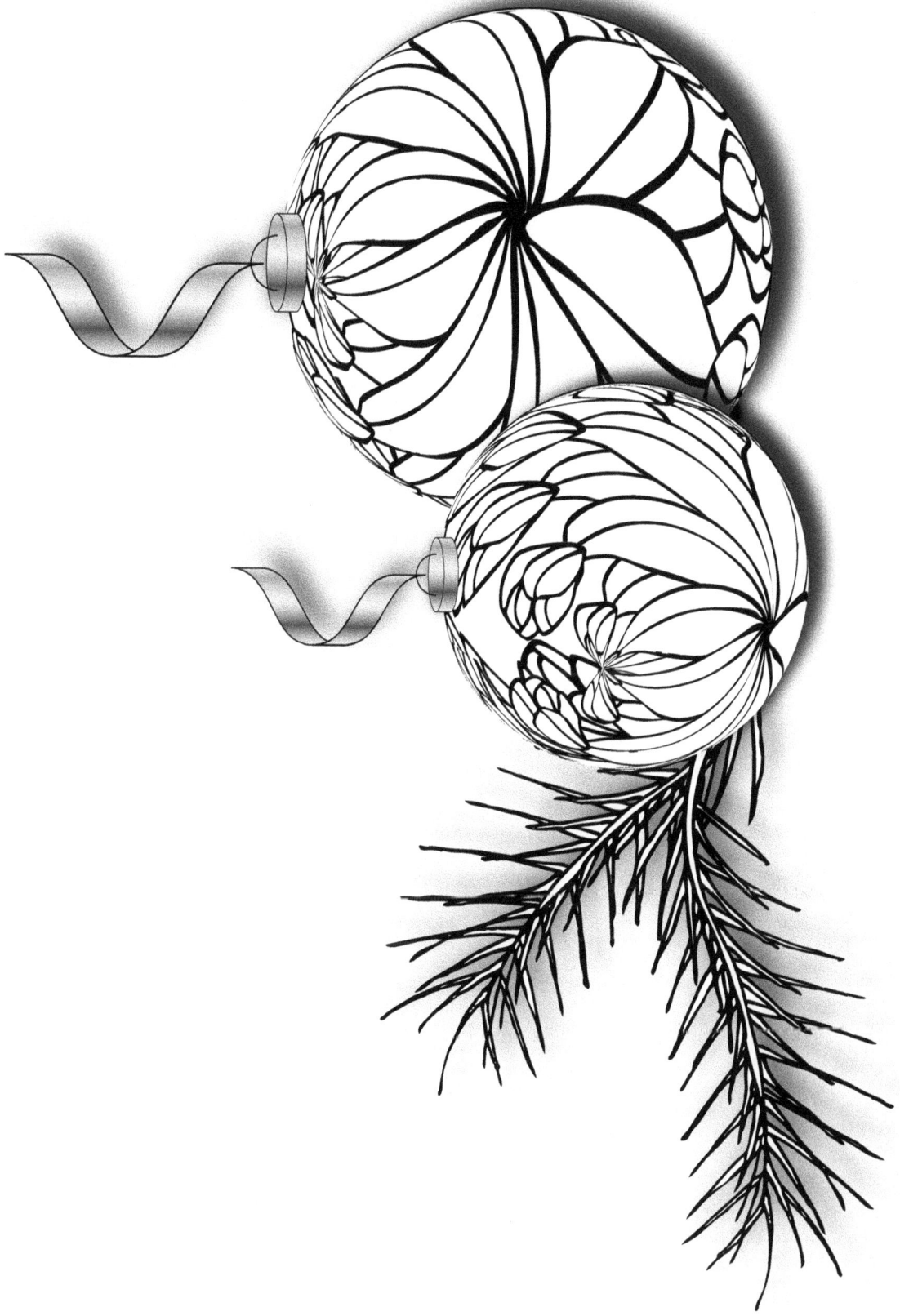

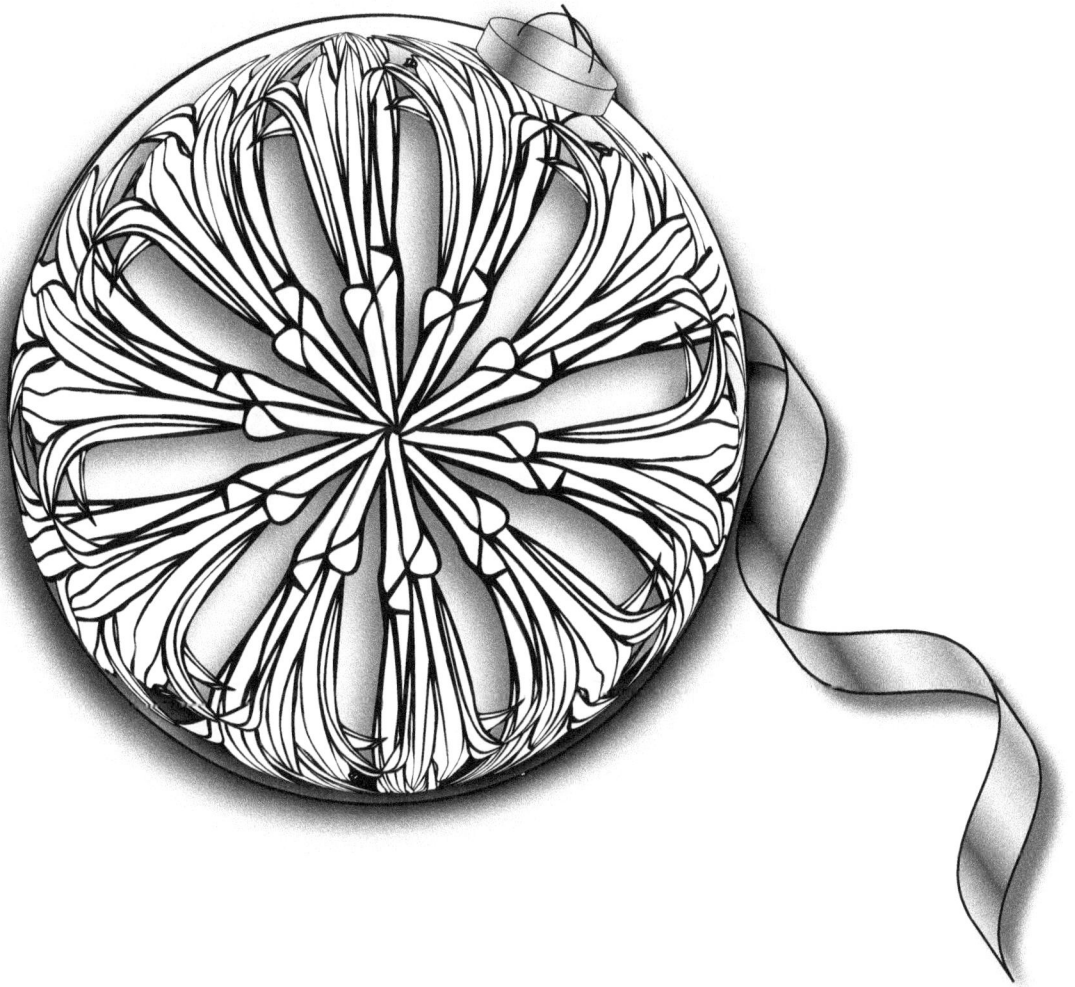

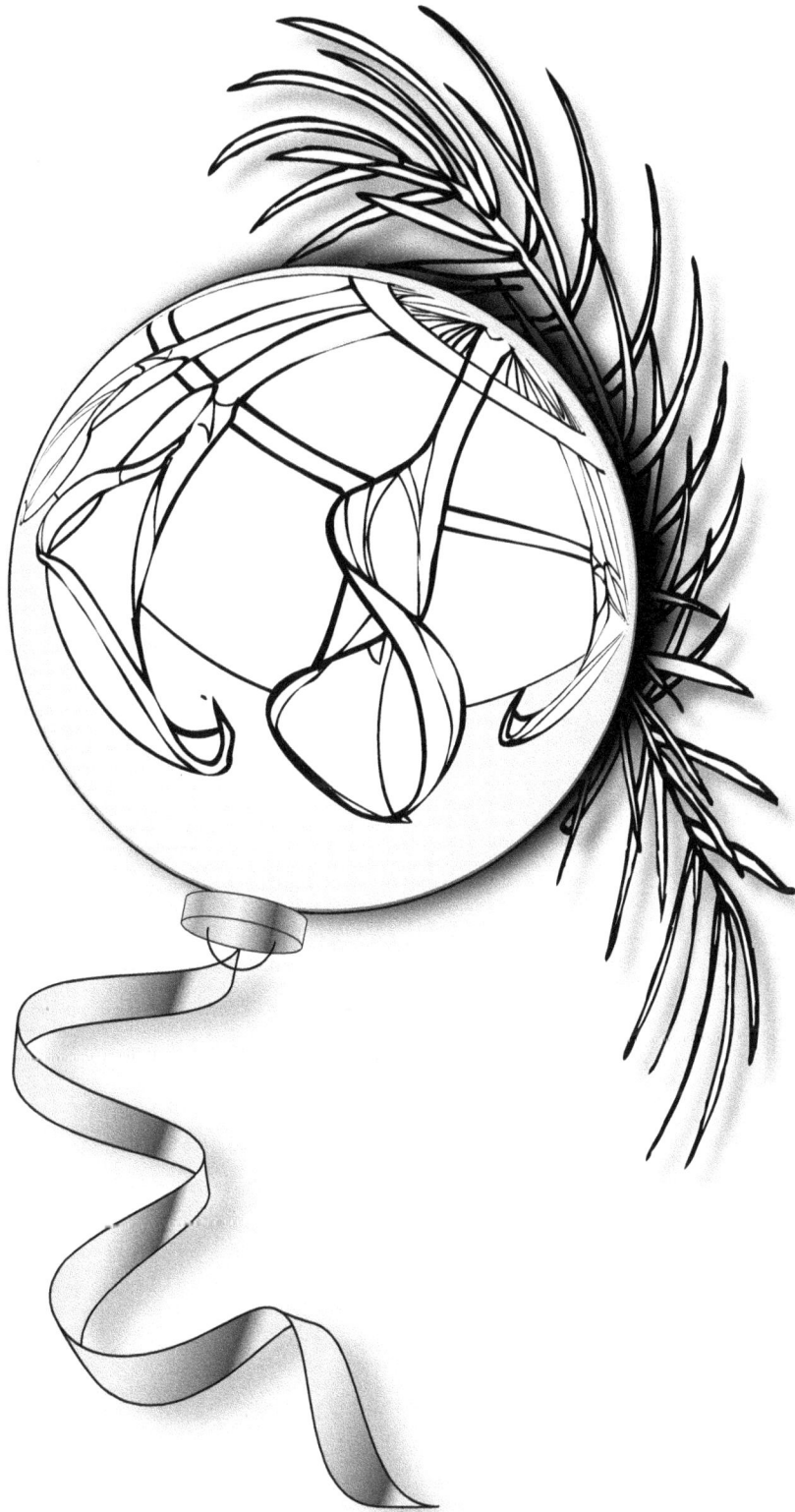

COLOR SWATCH TEST PAGE

Use this page to test and reference your colors

A Garden of Ornaments Coloring Book
© 2015 Paula Parrish

To learn about current and upcoming books,
and view colored samples of the works contained herein,
please visit the author's website

www.lovely-leisure.com